THREE J'S APARTMENT

LONG STREET

GRANT AVE.

TWO SISTERS' MARKET

CIRCLE DRIVE

LIBRARY

# TRASH
# TROUBLE

**Written by Larry Dane Brimner • Illustrated by Christine Tripp**

Children's Press®
A Division of Scholastic Inc.
New York • Toronto • London • Auckland • Sydney
Mexico City • New Delhi • Hong Kong
Danbury, Connecticut

For my Fulton Elementary friends in San Diego
—L.D.B.

For my aunt, Edith Drew
—C.T.

Reading Consultants
**Linda Cornwell**
Literacy Specialist

**Katharine A. Kane**
Education Consultant
(Retired, San Diego County Office of Education and San Diego State University)

Library of Congress Cataloging-in-Publication Data

Brimner, Larry Dane.
 Trash trouble / written by Larry Dane Brimner ; illustrated by Christine Tripp.
    p. cm. — (Rookie choices)
 Summary: On a field trip to the Nature Center, Three J leads his second-grade classmates on a
mission to pick up as much trash as possible after they find a bird caught in a discarded lunch bag.
  ISBN 0-516-22547-2 (lib. bdg.)        0-516-27837-1 (pbk.)
  [1. Litter (Trash)—Fiction. 2. Refuse and refuse disposal—Fiction. 3.
Environmental protection—Fiction.] I. Tripp, Christine, ill. II. Title. III. Series.
  PZ7.B767 Tr 2003
  [E]—dc21
                            2002008259

This book is about **respect for the environment**.

Mr. Toddle blew his whistle.

"It's time to go," said Three J.

The Corner Kids finished their lunches and jumped up. Three J, Gabby, and Alex called themselves the Corner Kids because they lived on opposite corners of the same street.

7

Alex and Gabby picked up their trash and put it away. They ran to catch up with Three J. He was already in line.

9

The rest of Mr. Toddle's second graders lined up, too. Then they walked to the Nature Center to hunt for insects.

Everyone gathered around the guide. "Stay on the path," she whispered. "Insects sometimes hide under leaves, so keep your eyes open. But remember not to bother them. We just want to find them. We want to make a list in our Nature Notebooks."

13

Just then Alex saw something.
"Yikes!" he said. He pointed at
a lunch bag. It was moving this
way and that.

15

"There's something in there,"
said Gabby. "And it's alive!"

Everybody wondered what it
could be.

The guide reached down.
She lifted up the bag.

"Ooooo," everybody whispered.

17

It was a bird. It looked around, then it flew away.

Everybody smiled. They were happy the bird wasn't hurt.

19

"Trash is trouble," the guide said. "Sometimes animals get trapped in it."

Three J began to think. What had he done with his own lunch bag?

Then he remembered. "That bag could be mine," he said sadly. "I didn't throw away my lunch trash."

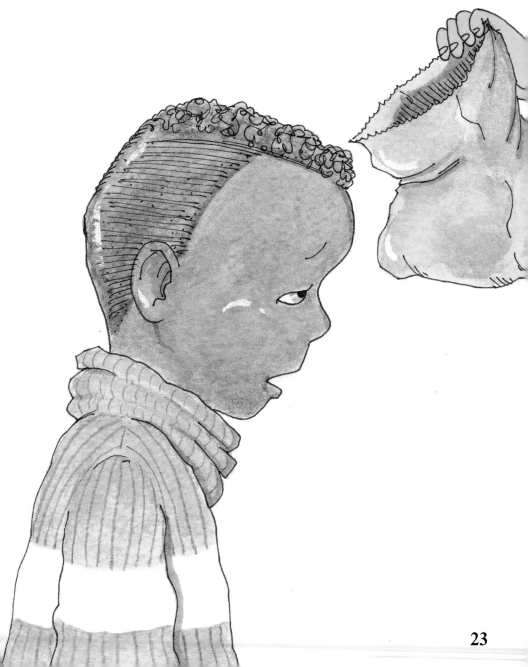

23

Three J looked around. There was other trash at the Nature Center. There was even trash floating in the creek.

"I have an idea," he said. "Let's clean up the Nature Center while we hunt for insects."

The guide smiled. "What a good idea!" she said.

Everybody agreed.

27

Back at school, Three J told
Mr. Toddle he wanted to do
more about the trash trouble.

29

The next day that's just what he did.

31

## ABOUT THE AUTHOR

Larry Dane Brimner studied literature and writing at San Diego State University and taught school for twenty years. The author of more than seventy-five books for children, many of them Children's Press titles, he enjoys meeting young readers and writers when he isn't at his computer.

## ABOUT THE ILLUSTRATOR

Christine Tripp lives in Ottawa, Canada, with her husband Don; four grown children—Elizabeth, Erin, Emily, and Eric; son-in-law Jason; grandsons Brandon and Kobe; four cats; and one very large, scruffy puppy named Jake.